TICKS

AN AUGMENTED REALITY EXPERIENCE

SANDRA MARKLE

Lerner Publications ◆ Minneapolis

EXPLORE INSECTS AND ARACHNIDS IN BRAND-NEW WAYS WITH AUGMENTED REALITY!

1. Ask a parent or guardian for permission to download the free Lerner AR app on your digital device by going to the App Store or Google Play. When you launch the app, choose the Creepy Crawlers in Action series.

2. As you read, look for this icon throughout the book. It means there is an augmented reality experience on that page!

3. Use the Lerner AR app to scan the picture near the icon.

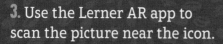

4. Watch insects and arachnids come alive with augmented reality!

TABLE OF CONTENTS

AN ARACHNID'S WORLD

Welcome to the world of arachnids (ah-RACK-nidz). Arachnids have jointed legs and a stiff exoskeleton. Their bodies are divided into two segments. They live almost everywhere on Earth. Some are even found in Antarctica.

A dog tick clings to a blade of grass, waiting for an animal to come near.

Most arachnids, including ticks, have eight legs and no wings. Ticks are parasites that eat by sucking another animal's blood. When ticks suck blood, they may pass on diseases that can make people and animals sick, or even kill them. Ticks are little arachnids that cause big problems!

tick feeding

 A tick's body temperature rises and falls with the temperature around it. So it must warm up to be active.

OUTSIDE AND INSIDE

LEGS: sharp claws at the tip that help the tick hold on

HALLER'S ORGAN: helps a tick smell when a host is nearby

ON THE OUTSIDE

A tick's exoskeleton is made of many hard plates connected by stretchy tissues. The tissues let the tick's body bend and expand while the tick feeds. Look at this deer tick to discover other key features.

PALPS:
help a tick find
a host's skin

HYPOSTOME
(heye-POH-stohm):
a needlelike part
that stabs into
a host

EYES:
located between
the first and
second legs

ON THE INSIDE

Look inside an adult female tick.

PHARYNX (FAR-inks): muscular tube pumps food into the digestive system

BRAIN: sends and receives messages to and from body parts

GONOPORE: female reproductive opening

Approved by Dr. Thomas Mather,
TickEncounter Resource Center,
University of Rhode Island

HEART:
pumps blood toward the head. Blood flows throughout the body.

OVARY:
produces eggs

SALIVARY GLAND:
pours saliva and digestive juices into the wound site during a blood meal

SPIRACLES:
openings that help ticks breathe

GUT:
where food is stored and digested

SOFT AND HARD TICKS

Check out some of the key differences between the two main types of ticks—soft and hard.

SOFT TICKS

- The bodies are soft and leathery.
- The mouthparts are more easily seen from below than from the front.
- The saliva does not hold the tick to a host.
- Adults leave their host to mate.
- They may feed and mate a number of times before dying.

This is a soft bat tick. While it mainly feeds on bats, it sometimes feeds on humans and spreads diseases.

HARD TICKS

- The bodies are covered by a hard, shieldlike plate.
- The mouthparts extend forward from the head.
- The saliva is sticky and holds the tick to a host while it feeds.
- Adults stay on their host when they mate.
- Males die after mating, while females die after laying one batch of hundreds to thousands of eggs.

A hard tick's mouthparts stick out from the front of its body.

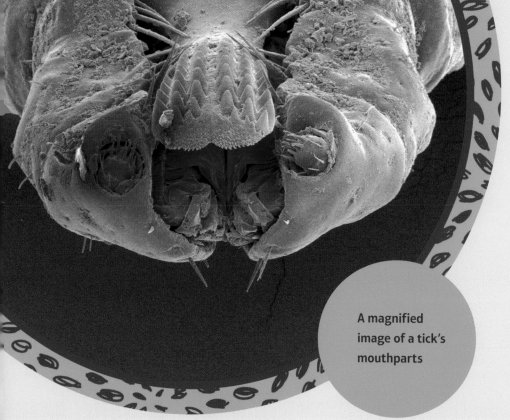

A magnified image of a tick's mouthparts

FEEDING TIME

Ticks feed on blood. Their mouthparts are designed to cut open a host's skin or covering. As the tick feeds, it pours out saliva. The saliva contains special chemicals that keep the host's wound from healing quickly. It may also contain microbes (tiny living things) that cause disease. The tick may have picked up these microbes during an earlier blood meal.

Soft ticks usually take smaller meals than hard ticks. That's because soft ticks can't swell as much as hard ticks. Before a soft tick starts to feed, the back of its body looks wrinkled. As the tick eats, the wrinkles unfold and the body swells. A soft tick may eat enough to increase its body weight about five to ten times. A female hard tick's weight increases nearly six hundred times during feeding.

Some of the chemicals in the tick's saliva numb the bite site. So it can feed without a host trying to remove it.

TICKS SPREAD DISEASE

A tick may suck blood from several hosts during its lifetime. If one host is sick, a tick may pick up microbes as it feeds. The microbes remain in the tick's gut. When the tick starts feeding on a new host, the microbes spill out of its gut. As the tick feeds, it passes some microbes into the host's blood.

Ticks might pass on bacteria that cause Lyme disease in dogs and people.

Lyme Disease

Symptoms: rash, flu-like symptoms, joint pain, nerve tingling, and trouble thinking clearly

Microbe: several kinds of *Borrelia* bacteria

Tick carrier: a number of kinds of hard ticks, including sheep ticks and deer ticks

Rocky Mountain Spotted Fever

Symptoms: fever, muscle pain, flu-like symptoms, and rash

Microbe: *Rickettsia rickettsii* bacteria

Tick carrier: American dog ticks and Rocky Mountain wood ticks

Tick-Borne Encephalitis

Symptoms: fever, flu-like symptoms, and later severe headache, trouble staying awake, confusion, and muscle spasms

Microbe: *Flavivirus*

Tick carrier: a number of kinds of hard ticks, including sheep ticks

BECOMING ADULTS

Like all arachnids, baby ticks become adults through incomplete metamorphosis. *Metamorphosis* means "change." A tick's life includes four stages: egg, larva, nymph, and adult. Larvae and nymphs look and behave much like small adults, but they are not able to reproduce.

During each life stage, ticks need blood meals to develop and grow big enough to molt, or shed their exoskeletons. Some kinds of hard ticks stay on one host their whole lives. Only females ready to lay eggs drop off.

Other kinds of hard ticks complete their life cycle on two hosts. The larvae feed on the first host and drop off to hide over winter. In the spring, they become nymphs and attach to a second host, where they become adults and mate.

A hard tick swollen with blood

Life Cycle of a Three-Host Tick (American Dog Tick)

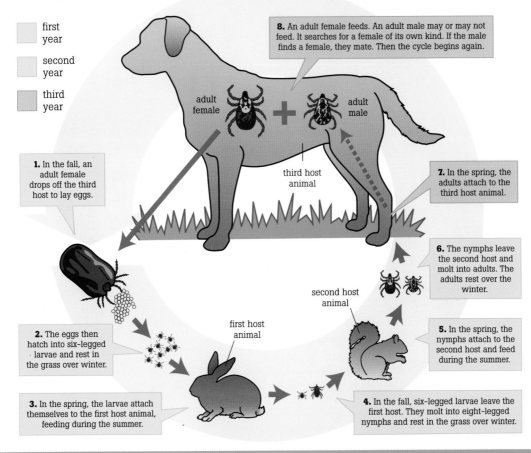

first year

second year

third year

8. An adult female feeds. An adult male may or may not feed. It searches for a female of its own kind. If the male finds a female, they mate. Then the cycle begins again.

adult female

adult male

third host animal

1. In the fall, an adult female drops off the third host to lay eggs.

7. In the spring, the adults attach to the third host animal.

6. The nymphs leave the second host and molt into adults. The adults rest over the winter.

second host animal

first host animal

2. The eggs then hatch into six-legged larvae and rest in the grass over winter.

5. In the spring, the nymphs attach to the second host and feed during the summer.

3. In the spring, the larvae attach themselves to the first host animal, feeding during the summer.

4. In the fall, six-legged larvae leave the first host. They molt into eight-legged nymphs and rest in the grass over winter.

Soft ticks and most kinds of hard ticks use three hosts. Eggs hatch on the ground, and larvae rest over the winter. In the spring, larvae attach to a host and become nymphs. Some nymphs find a new host right away. Others rest another winter and find a second host the following spring.

After nymphs feed on the second host, they drop off and molt. This time, they winter over as adults. In the spring, they attach to a third host. After feeding, soft ticks drop off to mate. Most hard ticks mate on the host during the summer. Then the females drop off to deposit their eggs.

A NEW BEGINNING

It is a late May morning in England. A female sheep tick stays still, waiting. Over time, the sun's heat warms her. She begins to crawl across the ground. Her body is swollen with eggs. These eggs have been forming inside her all winter long.

She picks a spot in the leaf litter. One by one, she deposits nearly two thousand eggs. As each egg leaves her body, it merges with a male reproductive cell. The female dies shortly after laying all her eggs. But inside the eggs, the baby ticks grow and develop.

This is an adult sheep tick. A sheep tick larva is as tiny as the period at the end of this sentence.

tick and eggs

Each tick egg has a tough outer covering.

On a warm day in late June, a female sheep tick larva hatches. She stays hidden in the damp leaf litter. Although ticks have a hard exoskeleton, their armor leaks. They tend to dry out quickly. To stay healthy, the female tick larva seeks a moist place to hide. It's also safer to hide among the bits of decaying leaves alongside her thousands of brothers and sisters. Birds, beetles, ants, and spiders will eat any tick larvae they find.

BLOOD MEALS

Before the tick larva can grow bigger and continue to develop, she needs a blood meal. Special sensors on her front legs let her detect movement and heat. Other sensors detect the carbon dioxide gas animals give off when they breathe. A rabbit brushes by the female sheep tick and several of her siblings. She crawls through the rabbit's hair, grips its skin, and snips open a tiny slit. She pushes her mouthparts into the wound and feeds.

This tick is nearly full and will soon drop off its host.

With her body swollen from her blood meal, the female sheep tick larva drops off her host. She crawls into damp leaf litter and stays hidden for nearly a year. All that time, she lives off her first blood meal. By spring, she's grown too big for her exoskeleton and molts. She is now a nymph. Though she looks much the same, as a larva she only had three pairs of legs. Now she has four.

When a dog walks past, the nymph grabs onto the dog's hair with her claw-tipped legs. Then she climbs up the dog's body and settles down to feed.

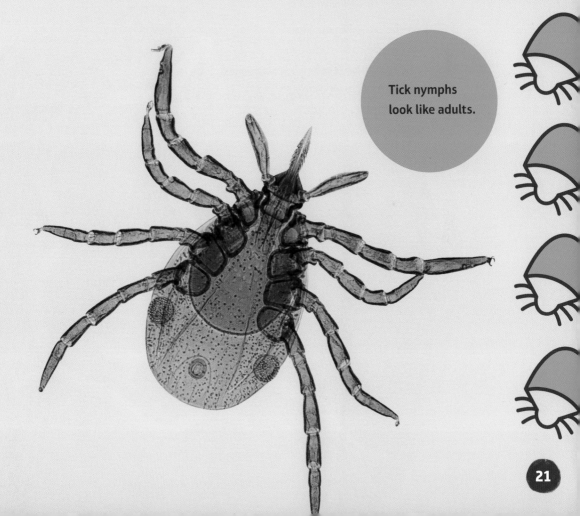

Tick nymphs look like adults.

She feeds until she's full. This time, though, her meal includes more than blood. The dog has Lyme disease, causing a fever and achy joints. About three weeks earlier, the dog was bitten by a different tick. That tick infected it with the *Borrelia burgdorferi* bacteria. When the tick nymph feeds on the dog's blood, she takes the worm-shaped bacteria into her gut.

Borrelia burgdorferi, **the bacteria that causes Lyme disease. People, dogs, horses, and many other animals can get Lyme disease.**

adult tick

An adult tick has just two purposes: find a blood meal and mate.

That fall, the nymph molts once more and becomes an adult. Then the young adult female finds a place in the leaf litter and rests through the winter. In the spring, she is ready for her third and final meal. When she finds a host, she deposits saliva and *Borrelia* bacteria into the tiny wound. She passes the bacteria to her host.

While adult female sheep ticks feed, they give off special chemicals. Like perfume, the chemicals spread in the air. Ticks can only mate with other ticks of their own kind. Any male sheep ticks sharing a female's host quickly start tracking her.

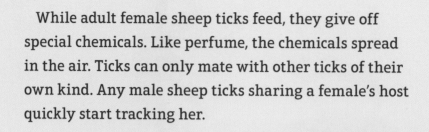

A sheep tick feeds on a harvest mouse.

A female sheep tick deposits nearly two thousand eggs before she dies.

Male sheep ticks don't waste time feeding. The adult males' mouthparts don't work well. They feed only a little, if at all, on this third host. They are on the host to find mates. If a male sheep tick finds a female sheep tick, he crawls under her while she's still feeding and inserts his male reproductive cells into her. Shortly after mating, the male tick drops off the host and dies. The female finishes her meal. Then she too drops off. It's time for her to rest for the winter while her eggs mature.

In the spring, before she dies, the adult female sheep tick deposits her eggs. The tick larvae develop inside their eggs. The tick's cycle of life continues.

PREVENT TICK BITES

Because a tick's bite can make you sick, follow these tips to protect yourself from ticks. Outdoors in grassy areas, wear socks, a long-sleeved shirt or jacket, and long pants. Secure cuffs tightly at your wrists and ankles. Spray the clothes you wear outdoors with an insect repellent containing a chemical called permethrin. Avoid sitting on the ground in leaf litter where larvae and nymphs often hide.

When you return home, check your body for ticks. Have someone else check your hair, the back of your neck, and your ears. If a tick is embedded in your skin, remove it using tweezers. Grab the tick where the mouthparts pierce your skin. Tug gently but firmly. Immediately treat the wound with antiseptic. Contact your doctor to find out if you need to take an antibiotic.

MORE ABOUT TICKS

Ticks belong to a group, or order, of arachnids called *Ixodida* (ick-ZAH-diduh). There are about nine hundred different kinds of ticks—hard and soft. All are parasites. They feed on blood they suck from other living animals. Scientists group living and extinct animals with others that are similar. So ticks are classified as

kingdom: Animalia

phylum: Arthropoda

class: Arachnida

order: Ixodida

HELPFUL OR HARMFUL?

Ticks are both, but they are mainly harmful. They're helpful because they provide food for other animals, such as birds. But they harm people and animals by spreading disease-causing microbes. The most common disease spread by ticks in North America is Lyme disease.

How big is an adult sheep tick? A female is 0.1 inches (0.3 cm) long. That's only a little bigger than a sesame seed. An adult male is slightly smaller.

TICK ACTIVITY

Follow these steps to see firsthand how ticks spread disease-causing microbes.

1. Pour water into two clear glasses. To one glass, add one teaspoonful of rainbow-colored nonpareils (cookie and candy sprinkles available in the bakery section of grocery stores).

2. Wait a few seconds for the nonpareils to sink to the bottom. Poke a plastic straw straight down into the candy bits. Cover the top of the straw with the tip of your index finger and lift. When you stop air from rushing down into the straw, you trap whatever liquid is inside the straw.

3. Place the straw in the glass of clean water. Take your finger off the top of the straw, and lift it out of the water. Look closely. You should see that a few of the nonpareils have been moved to the clean water. If not, repeat until you do.

This is the way ticks spread microbes from host to host. Microbes usually multiply so quickly that it takes only a few to cause disease symptoms.

GLOSSARY

adult: the final stage of a tick's life cycle. They are able to reproduce at this stage.

egg: a female reproductive cell and the first stage of the tick's life cycle

exoskeleton: the protective, armorlike covering on the outside of an arachnid's body

larva: the first immature, six-legged stage of a tick's life

microbe: a microscopic living thing, such as disease-causing bacteria

molt: the process of an arachnid shedding its exoskeleton

nymph: the second immature stage of the tick's life cycle

parasite: a living thing that lives in or on another living thing, a host, at the host's expense

saliva: a liquid that aids digestion

LEARN MORE

Arachnid Facts for Kids
https://kids.kiddle.co/Arachnid

Guyton, John W. *Bug Lab for Kids: Family-Friendly Activities for Exploring the Amazing World of Beetles, Butterflies, Spiders, and other Arthropods*. Beverly, MA: Quarry Books, 2018.

Lampke, Raymond J. *Lyme Disease: When Ticks Make You Sick*. New York: Lucent, 2019.

Lusted, Marcia Amidon. *Coping with Tick-Borne Diseases*. New York: Rosen, 2020.

Lyme Disease
https://kidshealth.org/en/parents/lyme.html

Markle, Sandra. *Jumping Spiders: An Augmented Reality Experience*. Minneapolis: Lerner Publications, 2021.

"Stop Ticks to Avoid Lyme and Other Tickborne Diseases"
https://www.cdc.gov/Features/StopTicks/

TickEncounter Resource Center
https://tickencounter.org/

INDEX

PHOTO ACKNOWLEDGMENTS

Image credits: Anest/Shutterstock.com, pp. 4, 5; KPixMining/Shutterstock.com, pp. 6, 7, 26 (top); Bill Hauser/Independent Picture Service pp. 8–9; Centers for Disease Control and Prevention Public Health Image Library/Jim Gathany, p. 10; Spok83/Shutterstock.com, p. 11; Gregory S. Paulson/Getty Images, p. 12; Maria Ogrzewalska/istock/Getty Images, p. 13; JPRFPhotos/Shutterstock.com, p. 14; Daniel Knop/Shutterstock.com, p. 16; Laura K. Westlund/Independent Picture Service, p. 17; Erik Karits/Shutterstock.com, pp. 18, 28; Bernard Lynch/Getty Images, p. 19; Bachkova Natalia/Shutterstock.com, p. 20; Ed Reschke/Getty Images, p. 21; RGB Ventures/SuperStock/Alamy Stock Photo, p. 22; nechaev-kon/istock/Getty Images, p. 23; Rudmer Zwerver/Shutterstock.com, p. 24; blickwinkel/Alamy Stock Photo, p. 25; Birute/iStock/Getty Images, p. 26 (bottom). Design Elements: Curly Pat/Shutterstock.com; Colorlife/Shutterstock.com. Augmented Reality experiences by Hybrid Medical Animation. Additional 3D models by VisualCenter/TurboSquid.

Cover image: Erik Karits/Shutterstock.com.

The author would like to thank Dr. Thomas Mather, TickEncounter Resource Center, University of Rhode Island, for sharing his expertise and enthusiasm. Also, Dr. Simon D. Pollard, University of Canterbury, Christchurch, New Zealand, for photo verification of the species that appear in this book.

Lerner Publications Company
An imprint of Lerner Publishing Group, Inc.
241 First Avenue North
Minneapolis, MN 55401 USA

For reading levels and more information, look up this title at www.lernerbooks.com.

Main body text set in Aptifer Slab LT Pro medium.
Typeface provided by Linotype AG.

Library of Congress Cataloging-in-Publication Data

Names: Markle, Sandra, author.
Title: Ticks : an augmented reality experience / Sandra Markle.
Description: Minneapolis : Lerner Publications, [2021] | Series: Creepy crawlers
   in action : augmented reality | Audience: Ages 8–12 | Audience: Grades 4–6 |
   Summary: "A tick cuts through a host's skin. It begins to drink blood as its body
   slowly swells. Learn about the life cycles of ticks with amazing augmented reality
   experiences and tons of creepy, bloody details"— Provided by publisher.
Identifiers: LCCN 2020012424 (print) | LCCN 2020012425 (ebook) | ISBN 9781728402703
   (library binding) | ISBN 9781728417936 (ebook)
Subjects: LCSH: Ticks—Juvenile literature. | Ticks—Life cycles—Juvenile literature.
Classification: LCC QL458.15.P37 M375 2021 (print) | LCC QL458.15.P37 (ebook) |
   DDC 595.4/29—dc23

LC record available at https://lccn.loc.gov/2020012424
LC ebook record available at https://lccn.loc.gov/2020012425

Manufactured in the United States of America
1-48256-48823-7/1/2020